THEOLOGIA

*being the treatise of Sa
Areopagite on Mystical 1
the first and fifth Epistles,* ......ated *from the
Greek with an Introduction*

by ALAN W. WATTS

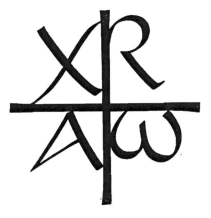

HOLY CROSS PRESS · WEST PARK · N · Y

MCMXLIV

FOREWORD

W HILE the purpose of this translation of the *Theologia Mystica* and of the first and fifth *Epistles* of St. Dionysius the pseudo-Areopagite is devotional rather than academic, it should be said here that with few exceptions it follows the text given in Migne's *Patrologiae Graecae*, vol. 3. This text has been compared with the earliest Latin version, by John Scotus Erigena, in Migne's *Patrologiae Latinae*, vol. 122. The translation comprises all his strictly mystical writings.

I should like here to express my thanks to the Reverend E. J. Templeton, S.T.M., Instructor in Greek and Hebrew at Seabury-Western Theological Seminary, for his careful checking of the translation; to Father Whittemore, Superior of the Order of the Holy Cross, for a number of valuable suggestions in the preparation of the Introduction; and to Mr. Adolph Teichert, III, for his generous assistance in the publication of the text.

ALAN W. WATTS

Evanston, Illinois.
Feast of St. Michael and All Angels, 1943.

INTRODUCTION

THE relation of God to the world must be considered in two ways. On the one hand, God is revealed in the world—in the divine humanity of Jesus Christ, in the faculties and virtues of the human soul and mind, in the beauty and power of the natural universe. On the other hand, God is infinitely greater than the world, and so differs from it in kind and degree that no creaturely image or form can possibly give any true idea of His greatness, His holiness and His essential Self. God reveals Himself to us, and yet remains infinitely mysterious. He is something like things that we know, like a Father, like the humanity of Jesus, and yet, in Himself, He is quite other than the things we know and experience. He is as different, much more different, from the world as color is different from shape. A circle is different from a square, a beautiful shape from an ugly shape, only in degree; but the color red is different from the shape circle in kind, and as no color can be described in terms of shape, the essential Being of God cannot be described in terms of any created thing. We can form rather less of a true idea of God's essence than a man born blind can form a true picture of a radiant sunrise.

By itself this truth might lead us to wrong conclusions, for it is equally true that we are given a correct idea of God's nature in Jesus Christ. Yet this is as if someone tried to reveal the beauty of color to a blind man by means of beautiful sound. Jesus is, as it were, the glorious sound of God's light; for the sound and the light (or color) have in common the quality of beauty God and the humanity of Jesus have in common the qualities of perfect goodness, holiness and love, and as we might represent the beauty of the sunrise to the blind man by beautiful music, so God represents to us the beauty of His transcendent nature by the beauty of His Incarnate Word. Though the blind man cannot realize what the sunrise actually looks like, he can know positively and surely that it is incomparably beautiful.

These two truths underlie the mystical theology of St. Dionysius the pseudo-Areopagite, which is at the root of the whole Catholic tradition of contemplative prayer.[1] He teaches that there are two ways of

---

[1] Originally supposed to be St. Paul's Athenian convert, St. Dionysius was probably a Syrian monk of the late fifth or early sixth century His works were widely quoted and deeply respected by mystical and theological writers of the middle ages, and notably by St. Thomas Aquinas, who regarded them as of the highest authority.

4

knowing God, one according to the way He reveals Himself in the world, and the other according to the way in which He is infinitely other than the world. The first is the subject of his book *The Divine Names,* and the second of his *Mystical Theology.* Obviously the second way is much more difficult, but he maintains that in the end it leads to a truer understanding than the first because it is the way of contemplative prayer in which the soul rises above all creatures to the pure knowledge of God. But we must begin the spiritual life by the first way, for we require revelation, positive knowledge of God's nature and will, mediated to us in terms of human life. Such revelation is neither false nor misleading, but necessarily incomplete, for which reason the deepest knowledge of God that may be granted us in this life must be in other than creaturely terms.

His *Mystical Theology* is therefore based on the principle of God's transcendence. God as the Maker of all things, all virtues, all ideas, is pre-eminently greater and other than what He has made, and to know God one must seek Him ultimately in a realm beyond all kinds of ordinary knowledge, whether it be knowledge of the senses, of the mind, or of the feelings. For God who is the Author of sense, mind and feeling can neither be touched, known nor felt.

Whatever may be touched, known or felt is a creature and not God. God and His creation are absolutely incommensurable, in somewhat the same way as shape and color.

At first sight this might seem to be saying that between God as He is in Himself and His creation there is an impassable gulf, and that to know God as He is one must not only look for no information from ordinary knowledge but even get rid of ordinary knowledge. Some have tried to understand Dionysius in this way, as if he advised us to seek God through violent extermination of the activity of the senses and the intellect, as if God and the world were not only incommensurable but radically incompatible. According to this view, knowledge of God and knowledge of the world cannot exist together; to know God one must blot out all consciousness of creatures.

But this is an entirely false interpretation of his theology. Nowhere does he teach the Gnostic heresy that God and His creation are incompatible; for the whole theme of the *Divine Names* is the compatibility of the two. The analogy of color and shape will again help us to clarify his ideas, for color and shape are certainly not incompatible, save in the sense that an ugly shape is incompatible with a beautiful color.

6

Thus the world is incompatible with God only as disfigured by sin. But just because shape and color are incommensurable they can be perfectly united. We cannot unite perfectly a square and a circle, and in the same way there could be no perfect union of God and man if God belonged to the same order of being as man, if He were greater than man only in degree. But as there can be perfect union between the color red and a circle, God and the world can be united without conflict while remaining essentially different. Therefore God's transcendence, so far from removing Him from the world, is just what makes it possible for Him to be intimately present in it without any loss of His absolute supremacy and holiness. For God can be present in the world yet never limited or contaminated by it, much as the purity and intensity of a color can never be lessened by its presence in an ugly shape. The shape could writhe and contort itself for ever, and yet have not the slightest power over its color.

Our first knowledge of God is through earthly and creaturely things that are something like Him, but those who are called to the mystical life are never content with this kind of knowledge. They want God Himself, not some creature like God. At first, therefore, they try to capture Him in some form. Such a form may be an idea about God, for we find that we are assured of His presence by thinking of the various doctrines of the Church concerning His nature. For a time this satisfies, but after a while we find that we are using the doctrine to catch hold of God and make Him as it were our own property. And, then, because He wants us to know Him more deeply, He makes this way of knowing His presence not untrue but inadequate. He slips from our grasp. Or again, the form in which we try to possess Him may be some state of mind or feeling. We may have some minor order of mystical experience and try to work ourselves up into the same experience again and again, imagining that we can possess a sense of God by pressing the right psychological button.

But as we persevere in these attempts to hold God in some form, whether a sensible image or state of mind, we learn that in truth we cannot possess God at all. "What," asked von Hügel, "is a sense of God worth which would be at your disposal, capable of being comfortably elicited when and where you please? It is far, far more God who must hold us, than we who must hold Him. And we get trained in these darknesses into that sense of our impotence without which the very presence of God becomes a snare." Such attempts to capture the sense of God in some form are much like trying to catch the wind in a bag; what can be caught is not the wind but only stagnant air, for the God who is a Spirit can never be held. It is He that must hold us, bearing us up in His Spirit like leaves upon the wind.

All men seek God, even though they may not know it. They seek Him blindly as wealth, power or material happiness; going higher than this, they seek Him in the strict performance of a moral law, in some feeling of spiritual elation, or some sensation of a mighty Presence. But all these things Dionysius shows to be creatures of God and not God Himself. Those called to the higher stages of the spiritual life must pass beyond them, resolutely setting aside everything that can be known or felt, saying, "This is not yet God." But this does not mean that the contemplative must utterly cease to know and feel in the ordinary way; it means that he must cease to identify anything that he knows or feels with God. He goes on with his daily work and with his normal Christian duties, but he tries to maintain at all times a loving faith in the immediate presence of the God whom he can neither feel, see nor know. He walks through a darkness so far as his comprehension of God is concerned, knowing God as That which he does not know—as a glorious mystery.

This is no mere agnosticism, for the Unknowable Reality of the agnostic is not an object of faith and love. Mystery for the agnostic is mere absence of knowledge, but for the contemplative it has a tremendous attractive power. It draws him into itself like a vacuum, and he reaches out into this void in the simple faith that it is a void only to his human faculties, and in reality is filled with the living God. In one way this is a hard, arid and costly task, for he has to devote his whole life and being to the love of what seems to be a void, though by faith he knows that it is the hiding-place of the Most High.

But there are compensations, and at the last a great reward. For he understands that the presence of God does not depend on his willing, knowing or feeling it. He sees that God's presence is given quite apart from any effort he may make to feel it. To try to feel this given presence is to ignore the truth that God is here and now in all His fullness. It is like a bird flying in search of the air. But as a bird can fly up or down, left or right, because it is in the air and has no need to find it, so we can give ourselves entirely and joyfully to the work of each moment, whether it be chopping wood or praising God, because we and all that we do are in God. For it is through rejoicing in His possession of us, and not in trying to possess Him, that we come to a true knowledge of God.

Thus the contemplative begins to have a true awareness of God not by seeking Him as yet another form of experience, but by accepting His presence as given like an invisible color in every shape of experience. He can thus devote himself wholeheartedly to his work in the simple faith that God is as much with him when he is not specifically thinking about God as when he is. God, he finds, is as present with him as the present moment; he may be thinking of past or future events but he can never escape from the present moment, which seems to carry him along with itself even when his thoughts are not immediately concerned with it. God is with us and carries us forward through our lives in rather the same way, for as it is said in Psalm 139:

Whither shall I go from Thy Spirit? Or whither shall I flee from Thy presence? If I ascend up into heaven, Thou art there: if I make my bed in hell, behold, Thou art there. If I take the wings of the morning, and dwell in the uttermost parts of the sea; even there shall Thy hand lead me, and Thy right hand shall hold me. If I say, Surely the darkness shall cover me, even the night shall be light about me. Yea, the darkness hideth not from Thee; but the night shineth as the day: the darkness and the light are both alike to Thee.

"The night shineth as the day." This is the seeming paradox upon which Dionysius loves to dwell, for he speaks of the contemplative state as the "divine darkness," a darkness of the spirit which Christian mystics have always associated with that mysterious cry from the Cross, "My God, my God, why hast Thou forsaken me?" This darkness is the climax of the Purgative Way, which is less a preliminary stage of the mystical life to be passed and left behind than the constant and primary condition of mystical prayer. We are always in the Purgative Way, and in this life never outgrow the need either for the forgiveness of sins or for the purification of our knowledge of God. In purifying our knowledge of God we come to the point where He seems, to all knowledge and sense, to have forsaken us utterly. For we have purified that knowledge of every attempt to grasp God in sensible and intellectual forms, so that there is nothing left to know in any ordinary sense of the word, save what may be known by simple faith in the truths which God has revealed about Himself. This darkness is as far as Dionysius takes us, for words can go no further except to say with him that the divine darkness "overfills our unseeing minds with splendors of transcendent beauty." After purgation comes illumination, for God takes possession of the soul when all its faculties are surrendered to Him, and no longer strive to make Him their own property.

The apparent paradox of a night which shines as the day is unthinkable without belief in a living God who acts and exists independently of our knowledge of Him. People of timid faith feel subconsciously that apart from some image of God in their minds there might be no God at all. Their God tends to be subjective and even idolatrous for they are putting faith in a mental or emotional image of their own making. They dare not reach out into the void beyond such images and feelings, fearing that God might not after all be there. Some such fear haunts almost all of us, for which reason, while it may sound simple, the complete abandonment of ourselves to this divine darkness is no easy matter. It means the abandonment of ultimate faith in all creatures whatsoever, whether they are objective people and things or subjective thoughts and feelings.

Some people regard this quest for knowledge of God in the divine darkness as a "tragic accident of Christian thought," a way of pure negation that denies all interest in creative life, fitted only for hermits who have a dismal delight in contemplating mere emptiness. But Dionysius's mysticism is negative only in the sense that the Cross and sacrificial death is negative. For this negative way of prayer is based on implicit trust in the existence of a positively excellent and glorious God who is only negative in so far as His glory cannot be described directly in any human terms. The divine darkness is a spiritual death out of which comes a resplendent life, because through dying to himself the individual is taken over and lived by God. He returns to the creative work of living and attends to it with the power of God in his body and soul, for "I live; yet no longer I, but Christ liveth in me."

The divine darkness can seem a negative and dismal goal only when there is lack of faith in the objective though invisible reality of a God who will mysteriously emerge from that darkness and fire the mystic with His own creative life. To the doubting mind it may seem incredible that the glory of God can come out of such emptiness. But it can for the simple reason that this glory is not of our own making, and that God will give it to those who do not try to substitute for it the visions of their own imaginations. Truly, "the desert shall rejoice and blossom as the rose." This negative way of Dionysian mysticism is, then, the central Christian mystery of "as dying, and, behold, we live." It is like the chry-

14

salis tomb, passing through which the grub becomes gloriously winged. For the mystical life follows the primal Christian pattern of Him who was crucified, dead and buried, yet rose again in a transfigured body, full of the glory of God.

According to St. Dionysius, contemplation is that high order of prayer in which the soul draws near to the very essence of God in a divine darkness which neither sense, thought nor feeling can penetrate. The power so to outdistance our own faculties of perception in the approach to God is only given to those whom God calls. While the possession of such a vocation is not necessarily a sign of great holiness, the very nature of the contemplative work demands that complete dedication of the self to God in which holiness consists. Others who have not this vocation and know little or nothing of mystical prayer may arrive at a holiness as great as that of the mystic in a purely active life of service and charity. We cannot say how many souls are called to the contemplative work; but not all souls are called, for which reason those who are able to use this order of prayer must not despise or belittle the other and more ordinary ways of prayer, or consider themselves more holy than those who cannot use it. For the ways to God are as many as the lives of men.

No infallible rules can be laid down for determining whether or not a soul is called to this prayer, but those who feel drawn to it would do well to consult an experienced director and watch out for certain temptations. Contemplatives are sometimes accused of being lazy people who like to sit and think about nothing, and a false idea of the contemplative work may indeed attract those who simply cannot be bothered with the more formal disciplines of prayer and meditation. The work of contemplation may also attract those who wish to pride themselves upon their spiritual superiority, since mystical writers are accustomed to speak of it as a "high" and "sublime" type of prayer. Such a motive simply nullifies the work. Yet only rarely is a soul free from this kind of pride, for which reason those drawn to contemplation must, of all people, constantly search for it in themselves and lay it before God for His forgiveness.

Contemplation is advisedly called a work, for it is no mere basking in the light of vague aspirations and "lofty" sentiments; it is rather a journey through a desert, bereft of most of the emotional and intellectual consolations of other kinds of prayer. It is a work because it requires a much greater degree of concentration, for the will has to leave behind the convenient props of verbal prayer and discursive meditation, and direct itself into the divine darkness with a single act of love and faith. Thus it should not be undertaken unless the soul feels positively and genuinely unable to use these other forms of prayer with spiritual benefit.

Strictly speaking, contemplative prayer is prayer of the will. For if we say that the human soul has the four faculties of sensation, intellect, feeling and will, vocal prayer, in which we use the sensible forms of definite words or such external aids as the rosary, is prayer through the faculty of sensation. This is usually the easiest form of prayer for the beginner. Next we rise to mental prayer, or discursive meditation, which is prayer through the faculty of the intellect, in which we ponder various divine truths or images in the thinking mind. Following this, the faculty of feeling comes into play as affective prayer, in which we feel about those truths rather than think about them. Instead of thinking love towards God, we feel love towards Him, and this feeling may express itself in short ejaculatory sentences or phrases of adoration and praise. But at last the diverse sensations of vocal prayer, the diverse thoughts of mental prayer, and the diverse feelings of affective prayer become a single and simplified act of the will, as if many shapes and colors were merged into a pure white light. For the will is the central and all-determining faculty of the soul, and in contemplative prayer we simply will towards God. For God is no longer conceived in the form of an image arousing sensations, thoughts or feelings; God is now known as One who can neither be sensed, thought nor felt; He is a mystery, a divine darkness, to be loved in faith by a pure act of will. Only the will can approach a God who is no longer to be conceived in some creaturely form about which we can have sensations, thoughts and feelings. All these lesser faculties find the divine darkness a total void which renders them impotent. But the will can reach out into that darkness, moved by the simple faith that the transcendent, infinitely lovable God is there by virtue of His own power, which is wholly independent of our thinking and knowing.

Thus contemplative prayer begins with what is sometimes called the "prayer of quiet" or the "prayer of simple regard," the latter term qualifying the former and showing us that contemplation is not a state of pure quiescence. The term "prayer of quiet" refers to the quiescence of the sensations, thoughts and feelings, but the term "simple regard" refers to an intense activity in that center of consciousness which underlies these three faculties. But this activity is not diversified. In sensing, thinking and feeling our psychological activity is relatively complex, embracing a diversity of objects, impressions or ideas. The light-beam of consciousness is diffused and moves from one object, or part of an object, to another. In the pure willing of contemplation the beam is less diffused, more intensified, and is brought to rest upon a single point. Activity ceases only in regard to the movement of the beam, but not in regard to the intensity of light.

It is particularly important to remember this principle because one of the great dangers attending this work is the temptation to pure quietism and a wholly negative and abstract view of God. Quietism may take one or both of two forms. It may be the notion that in prayer the soul should be completely inactive, abandoning even the direction of the will to God in love and faith. It may also be the notion that the contemplative should refrain as far as possible from every kind of active work, even the fulfilment of charitable duties and the active disciplines of the religious life. Now there are times when contemplation seems to involve a complete passivity of will, but this passivity is apparent only. The will has been utterly taken over by the will of God and experiences a great peace. Yet the sense of ease and peace is the result, not of complete inaction, but of acting with the will of God which bears up the soul like a mighty stream. As to the avoidance of charitable and religious duties, it must never be forgotten that God gives us His power, grace and love to be used both bodily and spiritually. We are to worship Him in act as well as in thought, and to love our brethren in both act and thought, for "if we love one another, God dwelleth in us, and His love is perfected in us." (I John 4:12.)

Quietism, which makes peace an end in itself, is generally associated with a passive and negative conception of God, sometimes fostered by thinking of Him too much in philosophical and abstract terms. The philosophical theologians speak of God as pure Being or as the unmoved Mover, but this should not give us the impression that God is in a state of blissful inertia, passively awaiting our discovery. God is unmoved in the sense that no other person or principle moves Him; He is absolutely self-moved. Nor does He rest inertly and merely await discovery like so much buried treasure. He reveals Himself; He acts; He gives Himself to us; ourselves and all the universe are a part of His activity, for we are something that God is doing. The faith that God acts quite independently of us is essential for the spiritual life, for it is by this faith that we are able to recognize His presence as given, quite apart from our efforts to become aware of it. By this faith also we are able to know that the power and love of God bears us up in spite of ourselves, even before we begin to abandon ourselves to Him. It is this faith which prevents the conceit that in contemplation, in seeking union with God, we are doing all the work, for in fact we are really giving the entire assent of our wills to something which God has already done. We give ourselves to God, not forgetting, however, that we already belong to Him entirely and that in this sense our selves are not ours to give Him. The realization of our absolute dependence upon God is perhaps the most helpful factor in abandoning our lives to His will, for it tells us that we have nothing to lose save a purely imaginary self-sufficiency. To try to be self-sufficient apart from God is like pretending that we are held to the earth by our own strength and not by the force of gravity.

This is not the place to discuss the more technical details of contemplative prayer which must always be treated at some length because they will vary according to different people. It will therefore be nec-

essary to consult such works of the masters of contemplative prayer in the Dionysian tradition as the
Cloud of Unknowing, Fr. Augustine Baker's *Holy
Wisdom,* Walter Hilton's *Scale of Perfection,* and
St. John of the Cross's *Dark Night of the Soul* and
Ascent of Mount Carmel.[2] Even in these works the
technical suggestions are not of so precise a nature
as would be expected, for instance, in a textbook of
music or even in a manual of ascetic theology. For
the art of contemplative prayer cannot be com-
pressed into formulae or communicated in exact
prescriptions which when fulfilled will lead inevi-
tably to the desired result. Generally speaking, the
instructions to be given are of extreme simplicity,
but there is the greatest variation of their applica-
tion to individual souls, while the work itself is
naturally almost as difficult as the instructions are
simple.

The reader will find that most of these works

---

[2] There are also a number of excellent modern works upon the sub-
ject. A standard but somewhat ponderous work is Poulain's *Graces of
Interior Prayer* (London & St. Louis, 1910.) Saudreau's *Mystical State*
(London & New York, 1924) is a particularly sound and valuable dis-
cussion of the various phases of mystical union One of the best works
for introductory purposes is Hughson's *Contemplative Prayer* (London
& New York, 1935) to which should be added the various works of Fr
Bede Frost, viz., *Priesthood and Prayer, The Art of Mental Prayer,* etc
An extremely full and profitable discussion is in Evelyn Underhill's
Mysticism (London & New York, 1930.)

have a deceptive somberness, for the authors approach their subject with gravity and caution, and give frequent warnings of the crosses which the contemplative must bear. They are wise, for they do not want to encourage souls to enter the work foolhardily. It should be said, however, that this apparent somberness conceals a divine gaiety of spirit such as one will find in the lives of St. Teresa and St. Francis, for their faith penetrates beyond the darkness to the music, the love and the laughter of heaven whither "the Lord is gone up with a merry noise." "If," said Coventry Patmore, "we may credit certain hints contained in the lives of the saints, love raises the spirit above the sphere of reverence and worship into one of laughter and dalliance: a sphere in which the soul says:—

> Shall I, a gnat which dances in Thy ray,
> *Dare* to be reverent?"[3]

Here is all the holy frivolity of those who have ceased to be burdened with the seriousness of themselves. In the knowledge of their entire and inescapable dependence upon God, they abandon themselves to Him without reserve, finding that

---

[3] Quoted from *The Rod, the Root and the Flower* in Underhill's *Mysticism*, p. 438.

herein is the only true security and freedom. And loosed from the anxieties and cares of the world, their inward spirit is as jubilant as a bird soaring and circling in the vastness of the sky. But their sky is not far above them in space, nor does the solid earth give it any downward limit, for those who have faith in the omnipresent, inescapable God find heaven upon earth, and, in the soul's dark night and death to self, perpetual light and everlasting life.

ON MYSTICAL THEOLOGY

The Treatise of St. Dionysius
to Timothy

I. *Of the Divine Darkness.*

1. Thou Trinity beyond being,[1] * thou Godhead and most perfect Guardian of the divine wisdom of Christians, direct us to the height of mystical revelation, sublime beyond all thought and light; wherein the simple, absolute and immutable mysteries of Divine Truth are hidden in the translucent darkness of that silence which revealeth in secret. For this darkness, though of deepest obscurity, is yet radiantly clear, and, though beyond touch and sight, it over-fills our unseeing minds with splendors of transcendent beauty.

This is my prayer. As for you, beloved Timothy, exerting yourself sincerely in mystical contemplation, quit the senses, the workings of the intellect, and all that may be sensed and known, and all that is not and is.[2] For by this you may unknowingly[3] attain, in as far as it is possible, to the one-ness of Him who is beyond all being and knowledge. Thus

---

* See notes at the end.

through indomitable, absolute and pure detachment of yourself from all things, you will be lifted up to that radiance of the divine darkness which is beyond being, surpassing all and free from all.

2. But take heed lest the profane hear—those, I say, who cling to creatures, and imagine in themselves that nothing is beyond being, beyond existences, but suppose themselves to *know* Him "who maketh darkness His hiding-place."[4] If, then, the divine mysteries are beyond such, what shall be said of those yet more profane who conceive the underlying Cause of all in terms of the outward forms of things,[5] and assert that He exceeds not these impious and manifold conceits of their own making? In so far as He is the Cause of all things, we must needs impute and affirm of Him all their attributes; but in so far as He is beyond and above all, we must needs deny those attributes to Him entirely, yet not suppose that this affirmation and denial are contradictory, but that He Himself is before and above all denials, and beyond all negating and imputing.[6]

3. After this manner, then, the blessed Bartholomew says that Divine Truth is both much and very little, and the Gospel both wide and great, and yet brief. This seems to me a marvellous insight, for the excellent Cause of all things may be revealed

with many words, with few words, and with even no words, inasmuch as He is both unutterable and unknowable, because beyond being He stands above all nature. He is truly revealed without coverings only to those who pass above all things impure and pure, who go beyond all climbing of sacred heights, and leave behind all heavenly lights and sounds, and supernal discourses,[7] and are taken up into that darkness where, as the Scripture says, He truly is who is beyond all things. For not unmeaningly was the blessed Moses himself first bidden to be purified, and then to be set aside from the unpurified; and after entire purification he heard the many-voiced trumpets, and beheld a multitude of lights, giving forth pure and manifold beams. After he was set aside from the manyfolk, he went before the elect priests to the uttermost peak of sacred heights.[8]

But thus far he had not yet converse with God Himself, nor beheld Him, for He is without aspect, but saw only the place where He dwells.[9] This I take to mean that the most heavenly and lofty of things which may be seen and known are no more than certain images of things subordinate to Him who transcends all. Through them is shown His presence, exceeding all comprehension, standing on those heights of His holy places which may be known of the mind. And at times he who is set free of things seen and of things seeing, enters into the truly mystical darkness of unknowing, wherefrom he puts out all intellectual knowledge, and cleaves to that which is quite beyond touch and sight—the entire essence of Him who is beyond all. Thus through the voiding of all knowledge, he is joined in the better part of himself not with any creature, nor with himself, nor with another, but with Him who is inwardly unknowable; and in knowing nothing, he knows beyond the mind.

II. *In what manner we must needs be united with God, and of the praise of the Maker of all things, who is above all.*

We long exceedingly to dwell in this translucent darkness, and through not seeing and not knowing to see and to know Him who is beyond both vision and knowledge—by the very fact of neither seeing Him nor knowing Him. For this is truly to see and to know, and, through the abandonment of all things, to praise Him who is beyond and above all. For this is not unlike the art of those who hew out a life-like image (from stone), removing from around it all which impedes clear vision of the latent form, showing its true and hidden beauty solely by taking away. For it is, as I believe, more fitting to praise Him by taking away than by ascription, for we ascribe attributes to Him when we start from universals, and come down through the intermediate to particulars.[10] But here we take away all things from Him, going up from particulars to universals, that we may know openly the unknowable, which is hidden in and under all things that may be known. And we behold that darkness beyond being, concealed under all natural light.

III. *What may be affirmed of Divine Truth, and what denied.*

In the *Theological Outlines*[11] we have praised those things which fitly pertain to the theology of affirmation; how the divine and excellent Nature may be spoken of as One, and how as Three; how in accord therewith the Fatherhood of God may be explained, how the Sonship, and in what manner the truth of the Spirit may be revealed; how out of the incorporeal and undivided Excellence they put forth these three interior lights of goodness, and how in Himself and in Themselves, and in Their mutual and co-eternal propagation They remain together, nowhere going apart; how Jesus, while above all creation, may be in very truth of the substance of human nature; and whatsoever else that is set forth in Scripture we have explained in the *Theological Outlines*. And in the book *Of the Divine Names* we have told how He may be called Good, Being, Life, Wisdom, and Power, and whatsoever else concerns the spiritual naming of God. In the *Symbolic Theology*[12] we have told what divine names may be taken from things of sense, as well as what divine forms, figures, members, instruments, heavenly places and realms (may be spoken of in terms of sensible images.) We have also explained such other terms as are used as symbolic forms and sacred figures of the image of God (e.g., in the *Old Testament*), to wit the divine anger, sorrow, hatred, the inebriation and abandon, the swearing, cursing, sleeping and waking.

I think, too, that you have understood how the discussion of particulars is more lengthy than of universals; for it was fitting that the *Theological Outlines* and the treatise *Of the Divine Names* be less wordy than the *Symbolic Theology*. For the more we aspire to higher things, the more our discourse upon things of the intellect is cut short, even as, when we enter that darkness which passes understanding, we shall find not brevity of speech but perfect silence and unknowing. Herein speech descends from the universal to the particular, and as it descends it is increased in proportion to the multiplicity of things. But now, in truth, it ascends from the particular to the universal, and going up is withdrawn as it rises, and after the whole ascent it becomes inwardly silent, entirely united with the ineffable. But for what reason, you ask, do we ascribe as the divine attributes things universal, and begin our negations (concerning the Divinity) from things particular? Because in ascribing, to That which is beyond all, attributes which are more fitting to Him, it is proper to ascribe things abstract. But in taking away attributes from Him who is beyond all privation we take away what is truly most remote from Him. For is He not more truly Life and Goodness than air and stone? And, on the other hand, is He not more truly remote from dissipation and anger than He is unspoken and unthought?

IV. *That He partakes not of sensible things who is pre-eminently their Maker.*

We say, therefore, that the transcendent Maker of all things lacks neither being, nor life, nor reason, nor mind, yet He has no body; neither has He form, nor image, nor quality, nor quantity, nor bulk; He is in no place, nor is He seen, nor has He sensible

31

touch; nor does He feel, nor is He felt, nor has He confusion and tumult, nor disturbance of material passions; neither is He without power, succumbing to the contingencies of sensible things; neither is His light in any deficiency, nor change, nor corruption, nor division, nor lack, nor flux, nor is He nor has He any other sensible thing.

V. *That He partakes not of intelligible things who is pre-eminently their Maker.*[13]

Going yet higher, we say that He is neither a soul, nor a mind, nor an object of knowledge; neither has He opinion, nor reason, nor intellect; neither is He reason, nor thought, nor is He utterable or knowable; neither is He number, order, greatness, littleness, equality, inequality, likeness nor unlikeness; neither does He stand nor move, nor is He quiescent; neither has He power, nor is power, nor light; neither does He live, nor is life; neither is He being, nor eternity, nor time, nor is His touch knowable; neither is He knowledge, nor truth, nor kingship, nor wisdom, nor one, nor one-ness, nor divinity, nor goodness; neither is He Spirit, as we can understand it, nor Sonship, nor Fatherhood, nor any other thing known to us or to any other creature; neither is He of things which are not, nor of things which are;

neither do the things which are understand Him, as He is in Himself, nor does He Himself understand them as existing in themselves; neither is there utterance of Him, nor name, nor knowledge; neither is He darkness, nor light, nor falsehood, nor truth; neither is there any entire affirmation or negation that may be made concerning Him.[14] But on the other hand we make affirmations and denials of those things which are less than Him (and follow from Him); but of Himself we neither affirm nor deny anything, since He who is beyond all attributes is perfect and alone the Cause of all—beyond all negation the height of that which is entirely free from all and beyond all.

FROM THE EPISTLES

EPISTLE I, TO GAIUS THERAPEUTES

The divine darkness becomes invisible with light, and especially with much light. Knowledge[15] obscures unknowing, and especially much knowledge. Take these sayings in a sublime and not in a negative sense, and understand this loss (of light and knowledge) as in relation to that Truth which is transcendent.[16] For that unknowing which is of God eludes those who possess light and knowledge (of God) in terms of creatures;[17] and His transcendent darkness is concealed by every light and hidden to all knowing. And if anyone, seeing God, were to understand what he saw, he would not have seen God, but some one of His creatures that exist and may be known. But He that is set on high above mind and being, exists beyond being and is known beyond mind by the very fact that He is wholly unknowable and does not belong to the realm of being. And that perfect unknowing of the highest order is knowledge of Him who is above all things known.

The divine darkness is the inaccessible light, wherein God is said to dwell.[18] And this darkness is indeed invisible because of supernal light, and inaccessible because of light too great in transcendent intensity, whereinto each one is born that is worthy to see and know God. Such a one, by the very fact of not seeing and not knowing, truly enters into Him who is beyond sight and knowledge, knowing this, too, that He is in all things that are felt and known. At this he says with the prophet, "Such knowledge is too wonderful for me; it is high, I cannot attain unto it,"[19]—even as the blessed Paul is said to have known God in knowing Him as beyond all thought and knowledge. For which reason he says that His ways are past finding out, His judgments unsearchable, His gifts indescribable, and His peace passing all understanding.[20] This he says as one who has found Him who is beyond all, and has known this which is beyond thought—that He, being the Cause of all, is beyond all.

NOTES ON THE TEXT

[1] "Beyond being," (*hyperousios*). A more literal translation of the Greek would be "super-essential," a word of common recurrence in the Dionysian writings. It is not likely that St. Dionysius used the term *ousia* (*substantia*) in the sense of the Nicene-Constantinopolitan Creed, where God's essence or substance is understood as His very nature. It would be sheer nonsense to say that God is beyond His own essence. Nor are we to understand God as beyond being in the Thomist sense of the word *ens*. The thought is rather that God is beyond all objective and derived essence and existence, which is to say every kind of being that the human mind can conceive. God *is,* but not in the same manner that anything else is.

[2] The meaning is obviously to quit the senses, etc., in so far as the quest for knowledge of God is concerned. The would-be contemplative is not advised to become as unintelligent and unfeeling as a lump of stone, taking complete and final leave of his senses.

[3] Unknowingly. The term unknowing (*agnosia*) is one of the Dionysian key-words, meaning much more than mere ignorance or absence of knowledge. To know God by unknowing is to surrender the mind entirely to God instead of trying to possess God as a concept of the mind or an object of knowledge. The mind knows God by unknowing in the same way that the soul is saved by losing itself. To abandon the mind to the Void of the "divine darkness" in the loving

faith that God is there, is the equivalent of abandoning the body to a sacrificial death in the full faith that God is beyond the darkness of the grave. In either case the very act is accompanied by a mysterious sense of the peace and joy of God, which is why the darkness of unknowing is described as full of light.

[4] *Psalm* 18:11.

[5] Lit: "in terms of those things last in being (*ta eschata*)." The "last things in being" are those most removed, functionally but not morally, from God—i.e., particular, material objects. The strong Neoplatonic influence in Dionysian thought is apparent here.

[6] To negate and impute, affirm and deny, ascribe and take away,—these terms denote the two ways of knowing God, according to His immanence and according to His transcendence. To know God through His immanent self-revelation in creatures is, in Dionysian terminology, kataphatic knowledge; to know Him as beyond creatures, to approach Him negatively in the understanding that He is neither this creature nor that, is apophatic knowledge.

[7] Dionysian mysticism has no connection with the so-called mysticism of visions and "psychic experiences," pre-occupation with which can be one of the most misleading false trails that cross the mystic's path. This is not to say, however, that all such visions are inherently false. On the contrary, God does on occasion vouchsafe distinct visions of supernatural things for purposes of conversion or encouragement. But these are not the true end of the mystical

37

quest, which lies in the realm of essence and not appearance.

[8] *Exodus* 19.

[9] *Exodus* 33:18-23.

[10] Here again, the text is treating of the two ways of knowing God, for, according to Neoplatonic ideas, the creative, self-revelatory process begins from universals and works downwards and outwards to particulars. This is God's descent to man, but man's ascent to God works up from particulars, through universals, which are the highest created things, and beyond to the essence of God Himself.

[11] One of the supposedly lost works of St. Dionysius. It is possible, however, that the phrase *theologikai hypoty-poseis* refers to his treatises in general and not to a particular work, although in this chapter he clearly refers to other treatises by name.

[12] Another of the lost works. The reference here is unequivocal.

[13] This chapter may easily be misunderstood if it is not remembered that when St. Dionysius says that God is not reason, or power, or light, or goodness, he means that He is not these things as we are able to experience them with our created minds and senses. We have only seen and known created light and power, and goodness as it exists in creatures, and these created qualities are not God because He has made them.

[14] Created light or truth is the polar opposite of creature-ly darkness or falsehood, but God does not stand in rela-

tion to darkness and falsehood as its polar opposite, for this would degrade Him to equality with them. The goodness of God is therefore in no dualistic or mutually interdependent relation with evil, as is purely human goodness. Our created minds cannot grasp the mystery of evil because they cannot rise above dualism and conceive an order of goodness which is definitively *not* evil and yet is not the equal and opposite of evil. Because purely human goodness is the equal and opposite of evil it can have no final victory over it. But God has final victory over evil because He is not in a dualistic relation to it. Evil is creaturely, and the dualistic relation can be between one creature and another, but not between Creator and creature. The absolute and essential goodness of God has no opposite which can limit and condition it so far as He Himself is concerned. *Deo nihil opponitur.*

[15] This is a special sense of the word knowledge, the original term being *gnoses* (in the plural). Here again, it is not meant that God is obscured by ordinary work-a-day knowledge of people and things, but that (a) *gnoses* in the sense of so-called objective knowledge or visions of God obscure the genuine mystical knowledge (*agnosia*); or (b) that the mystical union is impeded by *gnoses* in the sense of conceptual notions of God adhered to as final and ultimate truth.

[16] The latter part of this sentence is a free rendering of the Greek *apopheson hyperalethos,* or "apophatize super-truly" which is impossible English.

[17] The text as in Migne does not make sense here, and the

translation given follows the text of the *Codex Dionysianus* and the Latin version of Erigena.

[18] 1 *Timothy* 6:6.

[19] *Psalm* 139:6.

[20] *Romans* 11:33; 2 *Corinthians* 9:15; *Philippians* 4:7.

CPSIA information can be obtained at www.ICGtesting.com
Printed in the USA
LVOW122002150513

333634LV00013B/196/P